Thoughts Journaled by

Mary Ann Khoury

Timeless Treasures
JOURNAL

Published by Harvest House Publishers
Eugene, Oregon 97402

ISBN 1-56507-509-9

Cover design features art by Sandy Clough
taken from *Timeless Treasures*
by Emilie Barnes with Anne Christian Buchanan

For information regarding the cover art, please contact:
    Sandy Clough Studios
    25 Trail Road
    Marietta, GA 30064

Designed by Garborg Design Works, Minneapolis, Minnesota

Printed in the United States of America

96 97 98 99 00 01 02 03 04 05 /QK/ 10 9 8 7 6 5 4 3 2 1

*Each person's memory enriches our heritage. Each person's
story is a timeless treasure that will be lost unless someone,
somewhere takes the time to preserve it.*

EMILIE BARNES

Do not store up for yourselves treasures on earth....
But store up for yourselves treasures in heaven....For where
your treasure is, there your heart will be also.

MATTHEW 6:19-21

*Inheritance is priceless. Heritage is a treasure.
Clear tracks left behind are the pathway for tomorrow.*

STU WEBER

I'll note you in my book of memory.
WILLIAM SHAKESPEARE

You have the special privilege of providing a link to that heritage for oncoming generations. Write about yesterday. Write about today, which will be history tomorrow.

LOIS DANIELS

A thing of beauty is a joy forever;
It's loveliness increases; it will never
pass into nothingness....

JOHN KEATS

Her plants, her books...her writing desk...were all within her reach...she could scarcely see an object in that room which had not an interesting remembrance connected with it.

JANE AUSTEN